Parenting Advice
to Ignore
in Art
and Life

Parenting Advice

to Ignore

in Art

and Life

by Nicole Tersigni
Foreword by Glenn Boozan

CHRONICLE BOOKS
SAN FRANCISCO

Library of Congress Cataloging-in-Publication Data available.

ISBN 978-1-7972-2217-2

Manufactured in China.

Design by Maggie Edelman and Wynne Au-Yeung.

Capri-Sun is a registered trademark of Capri Sun GmbH.

10 9 8 7 6 5 4 3 2 1

Chronicle Books LLC
680 Second Street
San Francisco, California 94107
www.chroniclebooks.com

For anyone raising kids
in this madcap world.
You're doing amazing.

Foreword

You'll never forget the important parenting milestones: your child's first steps. Their first day of school. The first time a complete stranger stops you in the middle of a Costco bathroom to explain how you're breastfeeding wrong.

It's a small comfort, then, to know that parents have been receiving this kind of unsolicited advice since the dawn of mankind. Famously, God's first words to Eve when she left Eden were, "Hey girl! I have this *really* great tip for sleep regression . . ."

No wonder such instances of infuriating parentsplaining have been captured by the greatest artists of our time: Michelangelo, Leonardo, Raphael, the other Ninja Turtle one. I only wish that this hilarious book had existed way back then. Exhausted moms during the Renaissance would have taken one look at it and said, "What is this? I'm a peasant; I can't read."

But you can read, which is excellent news for you, a person who is about to enjoy this fantastically funny book.

Seemingly every other book on parenting is titled something like *How to Avoid Raising a Felon* or *Dads: You Suck*. In this overwhelming smog of shaming self-help literature, Nicole's book is a breath of fresh air. Its relatability will make any parent laugh, and if there's one thing parents deserve more of, it's laughter. And alcohol. Honestly, if you have a child under four, I think it should be legal for you to snort ketamine. Whatever helps.

For all you parents, I know you're doing great. This is simply based on the fact that either (a) you were cool enough to buy this book or (b) you had someone in your life cool enough to get it for you. Also, you've read this far into the foreword of a book, who does that? Good parents, that's who.

In conclusion, I will leave you with my unsolicited advice on how to respond to people giving you unsolicited advice:

Tell them to get wrecked. Seriously. It'll feel great; I promise. Put your own spin on it: "Eat shit," "Kick rocks," "Bugger off." Try a "Bless your heart," if you're from the South. If you're not one for words, may I suggest an elegant middle finger? If all else fails, give me their address and I'll kindly send them their own little bundle of joy (*bundle of joy* is what I call a turd).

Love,
Glenn Boozan

Strangers

"That naked baby should really have a hat on."

"You should cover up while you feed your baby. You never know when a stranger might look through your private window."

"You simply must have more children.

It needs a sibling; only children are so weird."

"Frederick was a little freak until I adopted Isabella.

Now look at him! Wearing a top hat!"

15

"If you don't put your baby in a onesie that says 'spoiled princess' or 'future president,' how will we know if it's a girl or a boy?"

"Forgive us for interrupting your lovely day at the park, but that baby will never learn to walk if you always carry him."

"Isn't she a little old to be playing with dolls? When I was her age, the only toy I had was a full-time job."

"May I offer you some free advice?"

"No."

"If you want to lose that extra baby weight— oh, did you say no? Rude."

"Your daughters are making a lot of noise; wouldn't you be more comfortable getting your lunch to go?"

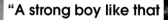

"It's none of my business—in fact,

it could not have less to do with me—

but if that baby naps all day,

they won't sleep at night."

"I have a lot of experience raising my lamb,

if you want any tips on how you're raising that child wrong."

Your

Family

"ck up your baby the second he cries."

"Even if you're asleep

on the toilet."

"Or not there.

"If you don't use a bottle, that baby is going to grow up obsessed with boobs. Like our perverted neighbor, Glen."

"Remember to sleep when the baby sleeps, that way you'll never get anything else done."

"We are here to hold the baby, not to do laundry or to cook."

"Here are some smelly gifts."

"Can you get us snacks?"

"Is it too late to change the name?"

"It's okay, baby. At some point your mother will clean the house.

I know there's nowhere for you to play, but she's doing her best."

"You better start with a routine now and stick with it.

Don't watch the clock."

"But having a strict schedule is important for babies."

"Loosen up."

35

"I breastfed mine until well after the doctor said to stop. I still give them an occasional squirt on their way out the door."

"Little boys should be outside, running around, eating dirt, punching other kids in the head . . . you know, boy stuff."

"What? I just asked if you're going to keep trying until you get a boy."

"You should stop babying this one; you don't want her to turn out to be an insufferable brat like the others. They can't hear me, can they?"

"You call that swaddling? If I wrapped a burrito like that at Chipotle, I'd get fired."

"I just think you two should have another one right away.

Her eggs aren't getting any younger.

I should probably tell her that."

41

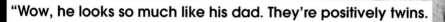

"Wow, he looks so much like his dad. They're positively twins.

Are you sure you had anything to do with it?"

"Your kid is such a tattletale. You should nip that in the bud.

I ate her ice cream, so what? She doesn't need all those calories."

"You should get him into pre-pre-preschool.

It's the only way to get into Harvard.

We're on six waiting lists."

"We never tell Mason what to do with his body. If he wants to hug your kid around the neck with his hands, you should let him."

"Not to brag, but our son was chosen for day care line leader. His teacher says he's so good at bossing the other kids around. What has your kid done?"

"Is this a TV? In your living room? I'm sure you've heard about how bad TV is for your kids' development. We don't even have one in the house. We're a board game family."

"We brought extra fruit because we weren't sure if your kid has ever had anything that wasn't McDonald's! Just kidding. Sort of."

"Ooh, looks like somebody's got a girlfriend.

Better start saving for the wedding now!"

"Cherish every single moment. Even when they're screaming at you and no one is sleeping and you're both crying and it seems like the longest day that will never end and it's just awful. Cherish. It."

"You have three kids? One feels like the perfect amount. You must be so tired."

"You let my son watch a cartoon movie that briefly shows period supplies? We'll have to play ball for hours to undo that damage."

53

"My baby isn't born yet, but I'll never let them run around barefoot."

"Music is so important for children's development. We formed a mother-daughter band. She says she hates it. And me. Haha. I'm positive she secretly loves it."

"If you didn't want my twins drawing little wieners all over your family portrait, you should have taken it down. I guess they're more artistically gifted than your daughter."

"We brought our dog this time because kids should know what it's like to have pets.

He doesn't bite too hard."

"If you homeschooled, your baby would be a farmer by now. My child grew these cherries himself. With the help of our gardener."

"I'm not judging you, but you're being a real helicopter parent."

"Your baby is literally playing with fire right now."

59

"Experts"

"You should feed your kid organic, homemade meals.

A single Cheeto will destroy his brain."

"You have to read the classics to your children. Less *The Cat in the Hat*, more *Cat on a Hot Tin Roof*. I know a kindergartner who has never even heard of Tennessee Williams. Can you imagine?"

our child endless amounts of love

ection."

"But r

"If you start potty training too soon, you will mess them up forever. But don't wait too long."

"Well, if the book says we need to have that specific, battery-powered, diamond-encrusted stroller, then we should sell a couple kidneys and get one."

"Here is a long list of things you cannot eat or drink or say or do or breathe or burp while pregnant. It's from my favorite book, *Helping Your Pregnant Dummy—Oops, We Mean Partner*."

"One of the worst things you could do while breastfeeding is to be stressed. So make sure you're getting enough rest and relaxation. Thankfully you're on your baby vacation. I mean maternity leave."

"...ed of bugs, they should confront ...d exposure therapy.

...a true-crime podcast."

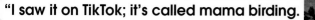

"I saw it on TikTok; it's called mama birding.

You prechew the food for the baby.

That's good, but more."

"Babies should wear shoes.
My sister's chiropractor's psychic
says it helps them walk."

"It might seem like he's interested in that simple toy, but bright colors and lights are better.

Remember, loud and blinky makes them thinky!"

"It says in this ad for organic baby clothes made from the finest handspun artisanal thread that you should only buy organic baby clothes made from the finest handspun artisanal thread. Unless you're a garbage mom."

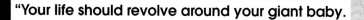

"Your life should revolve around your giant baby.

Being his mom is your only purpose now.

He really is enormous though, wow."

"Children should be seen and not heard. Always.

And I can hear you from all the way up here.

Not because I'm eavesdropping.

You spoiled *Stranger Things* for me."

Your Kids

"Grandma says if you didn't yell at us so much, you wouldn't have so many gray hairs."

"I'm only thinking of you when I ask to be carried.

I know you like to get places fast."

"If you want me to eat my fruits and veggies, you just have to ask nicely. Six or seven thousand times."

"That hat makes you look like a scary Halloween witch."

"If you really loved me, you would let Aunt Neigh and Peter Barker sleep in my bed."

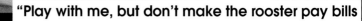
"Play with me, but don't make the rooster pay bills
and be mad about taxes this time."

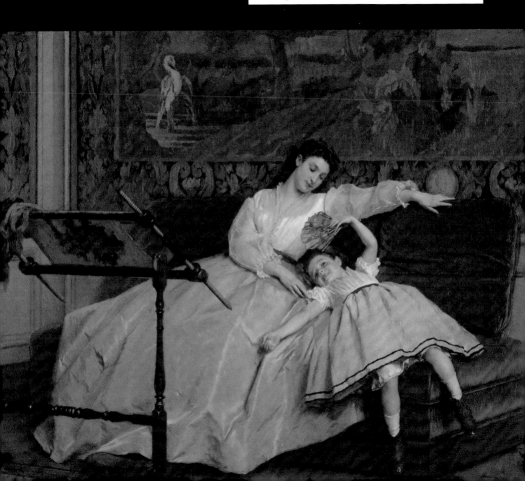

"But your room isn't clean either."

"You should've started yelling at us to get dressed hours ago if you didn't want to be late."

"No offense, but I can learn more about nature on YouTube."

"I am going to need *two* Capri-Sun drinks to make up for getting yelled at when I gave the dog mine."

"You can force me to apologize for barging in while you were pooping, but I won't mean it. If you wanted privacy, you shouldn't have had a kid."

"You can watch a million episodes in a row of *The Bachelor*, but I can only watch *one* episode of *Sesame Street*? I'm going to write to Elmo about this."

"We know you're trying to rest after playing with us all day, but you should play with us again instead."

89

"That's mine. Everything you have is mine."

Art Credits

Pg	Title	Artist	Location
11	**Adoration of the Shepherds**	Hans Leonhard Schäufelein	The Cleveland Museum of Art
12	**Virgin and Child with a Donor Presented by Saint Jerome**	Master of the Munich Bavarian Panels	The Metropolitan Museum of Art
13	**A Mother with her Children**	Cornelis Dusart	Artvee
14	**A Mother! How Odd!**	Gordon Ross	Library of Congress
16	**Madonna and Child with Two Angels**	Vittore Crivelli	The Metropolitan Museum of Art
17	**Madonna and Child with Saint Jerome and Saint John the Baptist**	Giovanni Battista Cima da Conegliano	The National Gallery of Art
18	**The Family**	Edvard Munch	Artvee
19	**Holy Family**	Bartolomeo Schedoni	Artvee
20	**The Holy Family**	Northern India, Mughal Court	The Cleveland Museum of Art
21	**An Elegant Family Portrait**	Jurgen Ovens	Artvee
22	**The Adoration of the Magi**	Quinten Massys	The Metropolitan Museum of Art
23	**The Holy Family with Saints Francis and Anne and the Infant Saint John the Baptist**	Peter Paul Rubens	The Metropolitan Museum of Art
24	**The Holy Family**	Michael Dahl	Artvee

26	Saint Anne with the Christ Child, the Virgin, and Saint John the Baptist	Hans Baldung Grien	The National Gallery of Art
27	The Holy Family with Saints Anne and Catherine of Alexandria	Jusepe de Ribera	The Metropolitan Museum of Art
29	The Holy Family with Saint Mary Magdalen	Andrea Mantegna	The Metropolitan Museum of Art
30	The Holy Family	Joos van Cleve	The Metropolitan Museum of Art
31	Virgin and Child with Saints and Donors	Giovanni Battista Cima da Conegliano	The Cleveland Museum of Art
32	The Adoration of the Magi	Giotto di Bondone	The Metropolitan Museum of Art
33	Virgin and Child with the Young Saint John the Baptist	Sandro Botticelli	The Cleveland Museum of Art
34	Virgin and Child with Saint Anne	Albrecht Dürer	The Metropolitan Museum of Art
35	Saint Anne and Virgin Child Enthroned with Angels	Niccolò Alunno	The Metropolitan Museum of Art
36	Holy Family with Saints Anne, Catherine of Alexandria, and Mary Magdalene	Nosadella	Getty Museum
37	Family Group	William Glackens	The National Gallery of Art
38	The Visit to the Nursery	Gabriël Metsu	The Metropolitan Museum of Art
39	The Pybus Family	Nathaniel Dance Holland	Artvee
40	The Newborn Baby	Matthijs Naiveu	The Metropolitan Museum of Art
41	The Holy Family	Joseph Paelinck	Artvee

42	The Holy Family	Francesco Zaganelli da Cotignola	Artvee
43	Andromache and Astyanax	Pierre Paul Prud'hon	The Metropolitan Museum of Art
45	Madonna Adoring the Child with the Infant Saint John the Baptist and an Angel	Lorenzo di Credi	The Metropolitan Museum of Art
46	The Holy Family with Saint John the Baptist and Saint Margaret	Filippino Lippi	The Cleveland Museum of Art
47	The Holy Family with Saint Anne and the Young Baptist and His Parents	Jacob Jordaens	The Metropolitan Museum of Art
48	Portrait of Antonio Ghedini and his Family	Giuseppe Baldrighi	Artvee
49	Holy Family with Saint Anne and the infant Saint John the Baptist	Bronzino	Artvee
50	The Holy Family	Bolognese School	Artvee
51	The Madonna and Child with Saints Elizabeth and Other Members of the Holy Family	Vincent Sellaer	Artvee
52	The Copley Family	John Singleton Copley	The National Gallery of Art
53	The Holy Family with Young Saint John the Baptist	Andrea del Sarto	The Metropolitan Museum of Art
54	Italian Peasant Family	François Alfred Delobbe	Artvee
55	Members of the Maynard Family in the Park at Waltons	Arthur Devis	The National Gallery of Art
56	John, Fourteenth Lord Willoughby de Broke, and His Family	Johann Zoffany	Getty Museum

57	Saint Mary Cleophas and Her Family	Bernhard Strigel	The National Gallery of Art
58	The Holy Family with the Infant Saint John, Saint Elizabeth, and Saint Anna	Vincent Sellaer	Artvee
59	Madonna and Child with Saint Elizabeth and Saint John the Baptist	Jacopino del Conte	The National Gallery of Art
61	The Holy Family with Mary Magdalen	El Greco	The Cleveland Museum of Art
62	Madonna and Child with Saints	Ludovico Carracci	The Metropolitan Museum of Art
63	Madonna and Child with Saints Jerome and Agnes	Giovanni di Paolo	The Metropolitan Museum of Art
64	The Holy Family	Johannes Paulus Moreelse	Artvee
65	The Holy Family	Pompeo Cerusa	Artvee
66	The Annunciation	Joos van Cleve	The Metropolitan Museum of Art
67	The Holy Family	Follower of Andrea del Sarto	Artvee
68	Mother and Her Family in the Country	Henry Fuseli	The Art Institute of Chicago
69	The Holy Family	Anonymous	Artvee
70	The Holy Family Dining Outdoors while Served by Angels	Frans Francken the Younger	Artvee
71	First Steps	Franz Ludwig Catel	The Metropolitan Museum of Art
72	The Holy Family	Raffaello Sanzio	Getty Museum
73	Virgin and Child with Angels	Bernard van Orley	The Metropolitan Museum of Art
74	The Adoration of the Child	Filippino Lippi	The National Gallery of Art

75	**The Return of the Holy Family from Egypt**	Nicolas Enriquez	Artvee
77	**Portret van Lady Smith en haar drie kinderen**	Francesco Bartolozzi	Rijksmuseum
78	**Mrs. Richard Brinsley Sheridan and Her Son**	John Hoppner	The Metropolitan Museum of Art
79	**Madonna and Child**	Andrea del Verrocchio	The Metropolitan Museum of Art
80	**The Railway**	Édouard Manet	Artvee
81	**A Mother with Her Son and a Pony**	Agostino Brunias	Artvee
82	**Child with Toys**	Auguste Renoir	Artvee
83	**Mother with Her Young Daughter**	Gustave Léonard de Jonghe	Artvee
84	**The Wife of Hasdrubal and Her Children**	Ercole de' Roberti	The National Gallery of Art
85	**Temptation**	William-Adolphe Bouguereau	Artvee
86	**Madonna and Child in a Niche**	Antonio del Ceraiolo	The Cleveland Museum of Art
87	**Madonna and Child**	Bartolomeo Montagna	The National Gallery of Art
88	**Lady Williams and Child**	Ralph Earl	The Metropolitan Museum of Art
89	**The Children of Nathan Starr**	Ambrose Andrews	The Metropolitan Museum of Art
90	**Madonna and Child**	Bramantino	The Metropolitan Museum of Art
91	**Fisherman's Wife Coming to Bath Her Children**	Virginie Demont-Breton	Artvee